P9-BIT-232

Shuli and Me
From Slavery to Freedom

A Storybook Omer Calendar

by Joan Benjamin-Farren

Shuli and Me: From Slavery to Freedom

Text and illustrations by Joan Benjamin-Farren
black pen, watercolor, collage, and paper-cut

Layout design by Kevin Turbitt

First printing
Published by Black Jasmine
Sharon, Massachusetts
www.shuliandme.com

Printed in Jerusalem, Israel
by Ayalon Printing
www.ayalonusa.com

Library of Congress Cataloging-in-Publication Data

Benjamin-Farren, Joan.
Shuli and me : from slavery to freedom : a storybook omer calendar / by Joan Benjamin-Farren. -- 1st ed.
p. cm.
Includes bibliographical references and index.
ISBN-13: 978-0-9788802-0-0 (alk. paper)
ISBN-10: 0-9788802-0-X (alk. paper)
1. Sefirah period--Juvenile literature. 2. Exodus, The--Juvenile literature. 3. Bible stories, English.--O.T. Exodus. I. Title.

BM695.S4B46 2006
296.4'39--dc22

2006034398

For Roselyn and Yossi

With thanks to Colette

In memory of Chip

The Children of Israel were slaves in Egypt. Being a slave was terrible, and they couldn't imagine being free. Once they were freed they found that freedom wasn't easy.

When they finally left Egypt, God showed them a cloud to follow by day and a pillar of fire to follow by night, but they didn't know where they were going. They didn't know what they would eat or drink. They didn't know how long it would take to get where they were going, or if something scary would happen on the way and they wouldn't get there at all.

This is a story about two friends who went on the journey out of Egypt.

Today the descendents of the Children of Israel count each day from the day of leaving Egypt (Passover) to the day of receiving the Torah at Mount Sinai (Shavuot). This is called 'Counting the Omer' and this book is an 'Omer calendar.'

Most of *Shuli and Me* comes directly from the Bible. Some of it comes from traditional stories found in the Midrash. More information about the Omer period, as well as the Biblical and Midrashic sources, can be found at the end of this book.

I was scared.
We were always scared, but this was worse.
Moshe said to put blood on our doorposts and stay inside.
We knew the blood would make our masters mad.
Then Pharoah said, "Go!" and we went!

פסח

Passover

Today we ran away from our masters.
We were so happy we danced.

היום יום אחד לעמר

Today is the first day of the Omer.

The second day we were still dancing.

היום שני ימים לעמר

Today is the second day of the Omer.

On the third day, Shuli whispered,
"When our masters catch us, they will punish us . . . "
I told her, "Pharoah ordered us to go. They won't come after us."
Shuli said, "They will too, they're mean."

היום שלשה ימים לעמר

Today is the third day of the Omer.

The fourth day, we thought we heard our masters' horses.

היום ארבעה ימים לעמר

Today is the fourth day of the Omer.

The fifth day was awful.
We smelled dust from our masters' chariots.
The sea blocked us in front.
Terrible wild animals were in the desert at our sides.

היום חמשה ימים לעמר

Today is the fifth day of the Omer.

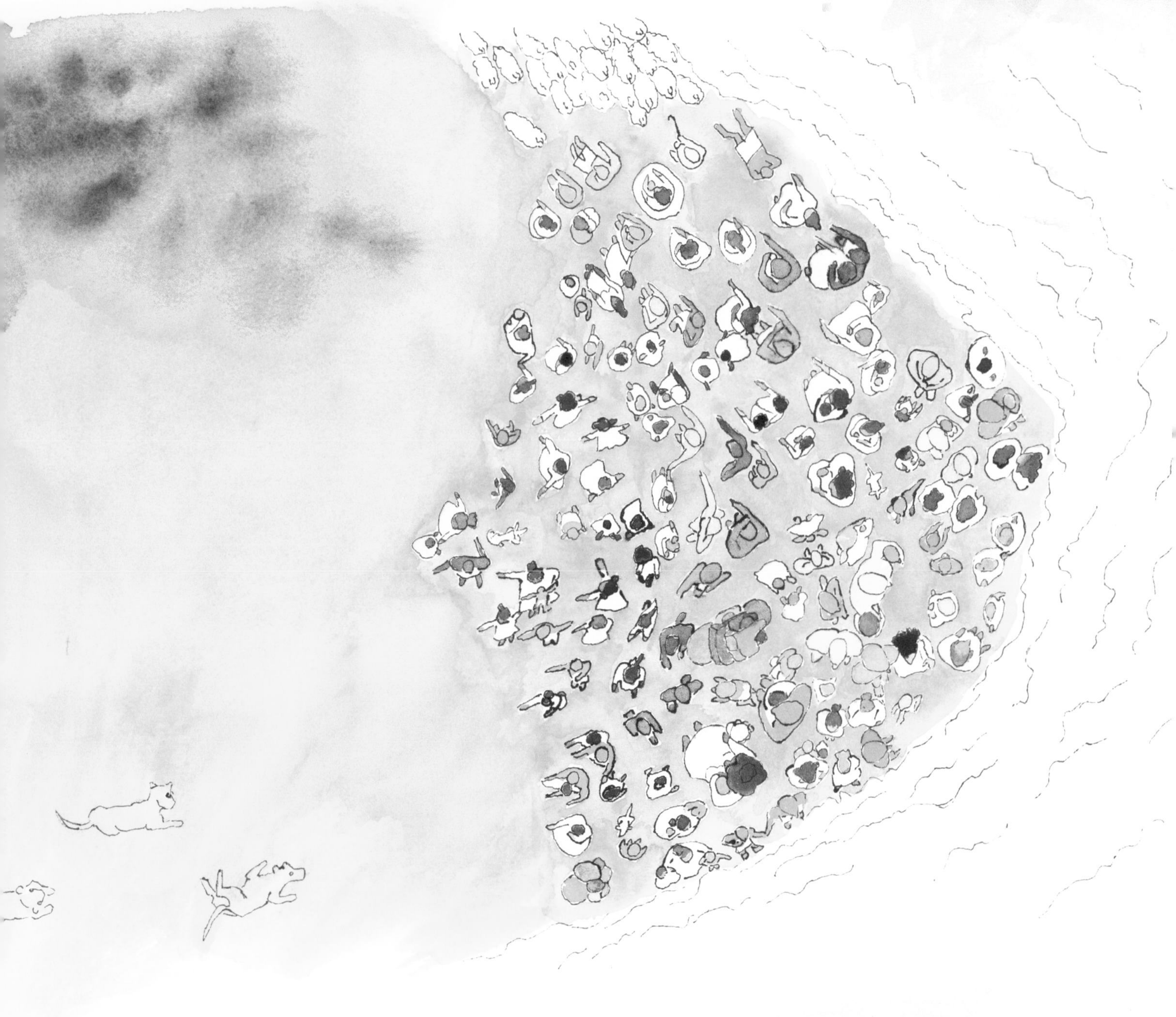

The sixth day we saw our masters, and they were mad.
We were so scared that we didn't know what to do.
Then Nachshon jumped into the sea, and the sea split open.
We jumped in after Nachshon.
Our masters jumped in to catch us.
The sea caught them, but it let us go!

היום ששה ימים לעמר

Today is the sixth day of the Omer.

On the seventh day, Shuli woke me while it was still dark.
She whispered, "Our masters are out there, waiting for us."
When the light came, we saw they couldn't hurt us any more.

היום שבעה ימים שהם שבוע אחד לעמר

Today is the seventh day, being one week of the Omer.

8

On the eighth day, we couldn't find water to drink.
We were hot, and we were thirsty, but we were FREE.

היום שמנה ימים שהם שבוע אחד ויום אחד לעמר

Today is the eighth day, being one week and one day of the Omer.

On the ninth day, Shuli asked, “What will we drink?”

היום תשעה ימים שהם שבוע אחד ושני ימים לעמר

Today is the ninth day, being one week and two days of the Omer.

On the tenth day, the grown-ups asked, “What will we drink?”

היום עשרה ימים שהם שבוע אחד ושלשה ימים לעמר

Today is the tenth day, being one week and three days of the Omer.

On the eleventh day, we found yucky water no one could drink. God showed Moshe how to fix the water to make it taste good.

היום אחד עשר יום שהם שבוע אחד וארבעה ימים לעמר

Today is the eleventh day, being one week and four days of the Omer.

The twelfth day was great!

We camped at a pretty place with twelve springs of yummy water and seventy palm trees.

היום שנים עשר יום שהם שבוע אחד וחמשה ימים לעמר

Today is the twelfth day, being one week and five days of the Omer.

On the thirteenth day, Shuli's dog had puppies.

היום שלשה עשר יום שהם שבוע אחד וששה ימים לעמר

Today is the thirteenth day, being one week and six days of the Omer.

On the fourteenth day, Shuli's goat had kids.

היום ארבעה עשר יום שהם שני שבועות לעמר

Today is the fourteenth day, being two weeks of the Omer.

On the fifteenth day, I got a baby sister.
Shuli brags her goat is cuter. She's jealous.

היום חמשה עשר יום שהם שני שבועות ויום אחד לעמר

Today is the fifteenth day, being two weeks and one day of the Omer.

On the sixteenth day, we played "Whompus" and I skinned my knee . . .

היום ששה עשר יום שהם שני שבועות ושני ימים לעמר

Today is the sixteenth day, being two weeks and two days of the Omer.

On the seventeenth day, my knee was better, and we both ran fast.

היום שבעה עשר יום שהם שני שבועות ושלשה ימים לעמר

Today is the seventeenth day, being two weeks and three days of the Omer.

On the eighteenth day, a scorpion almost bit Shuli.

היום שמנה עשר יום שהם שני שבועות וארבעה ימים לעמר

Today is the eighteenth day, being two weeks and four days of the Omer.

19

On the nineteenth, a snake almost bit me.

היום תשעה עשר יום שהם שני שבועות וחמשה ימים לעמר

Today is the nineteenth day, being two weeks and five days of the Omer.

On the twentieth day, Mom said, “Stay inside!”

היום עשרים יום שהם שני שבועות וששה ימים לעמר

Today is the twentieth day, being two weeks and six days of the Omer.

21

On the twenty-first, she let us go outside again.

היום אחד ועשרים יום שהם שלשה שבועות לעמר

Today is the twenty-first day, being three weeks of the Omer.

On the twenty-second day, we marched around camp.

היום שנים ועשרים יום שהם שלשה שבועות ויום אחד לעמר

Today is the twenty-second day, being three weeks and one day of the Omer.

On the twenty-third day, we drew pictures in the sand.

היום שלשה ועשרים יום שהם שלשה שבועות ושני ימים לעמר

Today is the twenty-third day, being three weeks and two days of the Omer.

On the twenty-fourth day, we played “Judges.”
I judged like Moshe.
I judged that Shuli was right.
I did great!

היום ארבעה ועשרים יום שהם שלשה שבועות ושלשה ימים לעמר

Today is the twenty-fourth day, being three weeks and three days of the Omer.

On the twenty-fifth day, Shuli judged.
She judged that her brother was right, not me . . .
I got mad at Shuli.

היום חמשה ועשרים יום שהם שלשה שבועות וארבעה ימים לעמר

Today is the twenty-fifth day, being three weeks and four days of the Omer.

26

...and on the twenty-sixth day, I was still mad.

היום ששה ועשרים יום שהם שלשה שבועות וחמשה ימים לעמר

Today is the twenty-sixth day being three weeks and five days of the Omer.

On the twenty-seventh day, Shuli and I made up.

היום שבעה ועשרים יום שהם שלשה שבועות וששה ימים לעמר

Today is the twenty-seventh day, being three weeks and six days of the Omer.

On the twenty-eighth day, the sign God gave us moved, so we moved too.

היום שמנה ועשרים יום שהם ארבעה שבועות לעמר

Today is the twenty-eighth day, being four weeks of the Omer.

On the twenty-ninth day, we camped by the sea.
We were hungry.
Shuli said, "I want bread!"

היום תשעה ועשרים יום שהם ארבעה שבועות ויום אחד לעמר

Today is the twenty-ninth day, being four weeks and one day of the Omer.

30

On the thirtieth day, something white and fluffy fell on the ground.

We asked, "What is it?"

Moshe said, "It's manna . . . bread." It didn't look like bread.

היום שלשים יום שהם ארבעה שבועות ושני ימים לעמר

Today is the thirtieth day, being four weeks and two days of the Omer.

On the thirty-first day, the manna fell again.

היום אחד ושלשים יום שהם ארבעה שבועות ושלשה ימים לעמר

Today is the thirty-first day, being four weeks and three days of the Omer.

On the thirty-second, more manna. It tasted like cookies to me, but Shuli said, “Delicious bread!”

היום שנים ושלשים יום שהם ארבעה שבועות וארבעה ימים לעמר

Today is the thirty-second day, being four weeks and four days of the Omer.

33

On the thirty-third day, it tasted like dates.
"Almond cake!" said Shuli.

היום שלשה ושלשים יום שהם ארבעה שבועות וחמשה ימים לעמר

Today is the thirty-third day, being four weeks and five days of the Omer.

On the thirty-fourth day, we agreed that manna tastes like grapes.

היום ארבעה ושלשים יום שהם ארבעה שבועות וששה ימים לעמר

Today is the thirty-fourth day, being four weeks and six days of the Omer.

On the thirty-fifth day, Moshe said, “Tomorrow is Shabbat.
There will be manna enough for two days.”
Until today there was only enough manna for one day.
Mom made a salad from ours, and Shuli’s mom fried theirs.

היום חמשה ושלשים יום שהם חמשה שבועות לעמר

Today is the thirty-fifth day, being five weeks of the Omer.

On the thirty-sixth day, Shabbat was hot.

היום ששה ושלשים יום שהם חמשה שבועות ויום אחד לעמר

Today is the thirty-sixth day, being five weeks and one day of the Omer.

37

On the thirty-seventh day, I was thirsty.
The cloud moved, so we moved too.
Shuli said, “I hate moving!”

היום שבעה ושלשים יום שהם חמשה שבועות ושני ימים לעמר

Today is the thirty-seventh day, being five weeks and two days of the Omer.

On the thirty-eighth day, the grown-ups yelled at Moshe,
"We're thirsty! Give us water to drink!"
Moshe walked far out into the desert.
He hit a rock God showed him.
Water rushed out.
Lots of water.

היום שמנה ושלשים יום שהם חמשה שבועות ושלשה ימים לעמר

Today is the thirty-eighth day, being five weeks and three days of the Omer.

On the thirty-ninth day, the Amalekites started a fight with us. Shuli worried that we'd lose and become their slaves.

היום תשעה ושלשים יום שהם חמשה שבועות וארבעה ימים לעמר

Today is the thirty-ninth day, being five weeks and four days of the Omer.

On the fortieth day, Moshe stood on a hill and raised his hands. We looked up at his hands and then looked way up and we won!

היום ארבעים יום שהם חמשה שבועות וחמשה ימים לעמר

Today is the fortieth day, being five weeks and five days of the Omer.

On the forty-first day, we talked about how bad it was to be a slave.

היום אחד וארבעים יום שהם חמשה שבועות וששה ימים לעמר

Today is the forty-first day, being five weeks and six days of the Omer.

On the forty-second day, we wondered when we'd get to wherever we were going.

Shuli grumped, "I think we're lost!"

I told her, "Shhh, we'll be okay, we're following the cloud."

Shuli grumped, "It's lost too."

היום שנים וארבעים יום שהם ששה שבועות לעמר

Today is the forty-second day, being six weeks of the Omer.

On the forty-third day, we took turns piggy-backing each other.

היום שלשה וארבעים יום שהם ששה שבועות ויום אחד לעמר

Today is the forty-third day, being six weeks and one day of the Omer.

On the forty-fourth day, we played freeze tag.

היום ארבעה וארבעים יום שהם ששה שבועות ושני ימים לעמר

Today is the forty-fourth day, being six weeks and two days of the Omer.

On the forty-fifth day, the cloud moved near a mountain.
Shuli roared, “I hate mountains!”

היום חמשה וארבעים יום שהם ששה שבועות ושלשה ימים לעמר

Today is the forty-fifth day, being six weeks and three days of the Omer.

On the forty-sixth day, Shuli said she hated everything, so we let her choose what to play.

She picked throwing rocks.

היום ששה וארבעים יום שהם ששה שבועות וארבעה ימים לעמר

Today is the forty-sixth day, being six weeks and four days of the Omer.

On the forty-seventh day, God told Moshe to put up a fence around the mountain.

We put up a fence.

Moshe said, "Wash your clothes." We washed our clothes.

Something was going to happen! Shuli said, "At last!"

היום שבעה וארבעים יום שהם ששה שבועות וחמשה ימים לעמר

Today is the forty-seventh day, being six weeks and five days of the Omer.

On the forty-eighth day, we waited
and waited
all day.

היום שמנה וארבעים יום שהם ששה שבועות וששה ימים לעמר

Today is the forty-eighth day, being six weeks and six days of the Omer.

The forty-ninth day was l o o o o o o o o o o o o o o o o o n g.

היום תשעה וארבעים יום שהם שבעה שבועות לעמר

Today is the forty-ninth day, being seven weeks of the Omer.

Today there was loud lightning and bright thunder on the mountain.

We heard God's words without using our ears.

"I'm scared," Shuli cried, "Something worse will happen!"

But nothing happened.

Everything turned out fine.

שבועות

SHAVUOT!

And it's still fine.

About the Omer period and how to use this book as an Omer Calendar:

The Omer period starts when it is dark outside on the day after Passover begins. You can find the date for Passover on a calendar or by using a computer and looking it up on the World Wide Web. Although the first day of Passover is not counted, it is included here so you can know when to start.

The Omer period is forty-nine days, which is seven weeks. Forty-nine days are numbered in the circle on the left-hand page. Larger balls in the frame near the circle represent the weeks, and the tiny balls are additional days. This reflects the phrase in Hebrew and English at the bottom of the left-hand page, which is the traditional statement of the counting.

On the fiftieth day from Passover is the celebration of Shavuot.

If you want to use this book as an Omer calendar you can start with Passover and move a book-mark each day as the days go by until you get to the forty-ninth day. If you read Hebrew, you can count in Hebrew, if not, you can count the days in English.

The counting takes place at night and there's a blessing to say each night before you count:

BLESSED ARE YOU, LORD OUR GOD, KING OF THE UNIVERSE,
WHO HAS COMMANDED US ON THE COUNTING OF THE OMER.

The Hebrew version of the blessing is available in Jewish prayer books.

Other things that happen during the Omer period:

The small circles at the bottom of the left-hand pages contain pictures about other important things that happen during the Omer period.

From Passover through the first seven days (in Israel only six are needed) the Children of Israel eat matzahs. There is a matzah in the small circle on each of these days.

The twelfth day (the 27th of Nisan) is *Yom HaShoah*, when we remember the Holocaust, a terrible time. There is a terrible scorpion in the small circle.

The sixteenth day (the 1st of Iyar) is Rosh Chodesh Iyar, the beginning of the month of Iyar. There is a new moon inside the circle as there is a new moon in the sky outside.

The nineteenth day (the 4th of Iyar) is *Yom HaZikaron*, Israel's Memorial Day. There are horns in the small circle because in Israel air raid sirens are blown to remember the soldiers who helped make Israel a free state.

The twentieth day (the 5th of Iyar) is *Yom Ha'Atzmaut*, a celebration of Israel's statehood. There is a Jewish star in the small circle as there is on Israel's flag.

The twenty-ninth day (the 14th of Iyar) is Pesach Sheni, when people who missed the Passover seder can make up the seder they missed. There is a matzah in the small circle.

The thirty-third day (the 18th of Iyar) is Lag B'Omer, which people in Israel celebrate by lighting bonfires. There is a bonfire in the small circle.

The forty-third day (the 28th of Iyar) is *Yom Yerushalyim*, which celebrates the unity of Jerusalem. There is a picture of Jerusalem in the small circle.

The forty-fifth day (the 1st of Sivan) is Rosh Chodesh Sivan, the beginning of the month of Sivan. There is a new moon inside the circle as there is a new moon in the sky outside.

The fiftieth day (the 6th of Sivan) is Shavuot, the time that the Children of Israel were given the Torah. There is Torah in the small circle.

Although Shabbat comes every 7 days, it is not indicated with a picture in a roundel because Friday night happens on a different date in the month from one year to another year.

About the story:

You can learn where in the Bible the ideas come from by looking at this list:

The counting of the days: "You shall count from the day following the day of rest, from the day you brought the sheaf of the wave-offering, seven full weeks shall be counted, you shall count fifty days to the day following the seventh week." Leviticus 23:15-16

Their clothes are from Egypt: "and the children of Israel . . . asked of Egypt . . . garments" Exodus 12:35.

PASSOVER: "Mark . . . the lintel and the two side posts with the blood . . . and no one shall go out the door until the morning" Exodus 12:22
"Pharoah said, ". . . Get out" Exodus 12:31

Day 1: "all the hosts of the Lord went out from the land of Egypt" Exodus 12:41

Day 2: "and the Lord went before them by day in a pillar of cloud" Exodus 13:21

Day 3: "Pharaoh's heart and his servants turned against the people" Exodus 14:5

Day 4: "all the horses and chariots of Pharaoh" Exodus 14:9

Day 5: "and they were very much afraid" Exodus 14:10,

Day 6: "the children of Israel walked on dry land in the . . . sea" Exodus 14:29

Day 7: "Israel saw Egypt dead on the seashore" Exodus 14:30

Day 8: "the women went out after her with timbrels and with dances " Exodus 15:20

Day 9: "they marched three days in the desert and found no water " Exodus 15:22,

Day 10: "they marched three days in the desert and found no water " Exodus 15:22

Day 11: "they could not drink of the waters of Mara, for they were bitter . . . and the Lord showed him a tree . . . he threw it into the waters, and the waters were sweetened." Exodus 15:23-25

Day 12: "they came to Elim, where were twelve springs of water and seventy palm trees" Exodus 15:27

Day 13: "not a dog shall move its tongue" Exodus 11:7

Day 14: "goats" Exodus 12:5

Day 18: They are looking, but can not find "scorpions" Deuteronomy 8:15

Day 19: nor can they get close to "snakes" Deuteronomy 8:15

Day 22: "in the first place went the flag of the camp . . ." Numbers 10:14

Day 23: "Moshe sat to judge the people and the people stood by" Exodus 18:13

Day 24: "Moshe sat to judge the people and the people stood by" Exodus 18:13

Day 25: "every small matter they judged themselves" Exodus 18:26

Day 28: "and they took their journey from Elim" Exodus 16:1

Day 29: "and encamped by the Sea of Suf" Numbers 33:10

Day 30: "and when the children of Israel saw it, they said . . . "what is it? . . . Moshe told them, this is the bread the Lord has given you" Exodus 16:15

Day 31: "and fed you with manna which you didn't know" Deuteronomy 8:3

Day 32: "and they gathered it every morning" Exodus 16:21

Day 35: "and on the sixth day they gathered a double portion . . . and he said, this is what the Lord said, tomorrow is the . . . Sabbath" Exodus 16:22-23

Day 37: "and there was no water for the people to drink" Exodus 17:1

Day 38: "and there was no water for the people to drink. The people strove with Moshe and said, give us water . . . and the Lord said to Moshe, hit the rock and water will come out of it" Exodus 17:1-6

Day 39: "then came Amalek and fought with Israel "Exodus 17:8

Day 40: "when Moshe held up his hand Israel prevailed . . . but Moshe's hands were heavy; and they took a stone and put it under him" Exodus 17:11-12

Day 41: "and Yitro rejoiced for all the goodness the Lord did for Israel" Exodus 18:9

Day 45: " Israel camped before the mountain" Exodus 19:2

Day 47: "and the Lord said to Moshe . . . let them wash their clothes and be ready by the third day . . . and you shall set bounds . . . that you not go up into the mountain" Exodus 19:10 - 12

Day 48: "and be ready by the third day" Exodus 19:11

SHAVUOT: "all the people perceived the thundering and the lightning and the sound of the shofar and the mountain smoking and when the people saw it they said to Moshe . . . let not God speak with us lest we die" Exodus 20:15,

The next day: "When you have eaten and feel full, then shall you bless the Lord your God" Deuteronomy 8:10

Other sources:

Much of the rest comes from stories told by the escaped slaves to their children, who told the stories to their children, who told the stories to their children, right down to today. These stories are mostly from the Midrash and the Talmud.

Day 1: "You have turned my lamenting into dancing." Psalm 30:12

Day 2: "Let them praise his name in the dance . . ." Psalm 149:3

Day 6: The man parting the sea is Nachshon. "He was the first to plunge into the wave (nachshol) of the sea." Midrash Rabba Numbers 13:7

They could reach into the sea for what they wanted to eat. "The daughters of Israel passed through the sea holding their children with their hand; and when they cried, they would stretch out their hands and pluck an apple or a pomegranate from the sea and give it to them . . ." Midrash Rabba Exodus 21:10

There were twelve paths through the sea, each of the twelve tribes went on its own path. Midrash Tanhuma – Beshallach 10

Day 30: The bread we see in the collage is from an ancient art work from Egypt.

Days 32,33, 34: "They found in the manna the taste of every kind of food . . ." Talmud – Yoma 75a

Day 44, 45: Miryam's well, the source for water in the desert, traveled with the Children of Israel. Shabbat 35:4

Day 42, 43: The water was so wide that "If a woman had to go to her friend who belonged to another tribe she would go in a ship." Midrash Rabba Numbers 19:26

Days 41, 42, 43, 44, 46, 47, 48, 49: When the people complained, "This is no place of seed or of figs" (Numbers 20:5), after they moved, it is clear that before this time fruit trees grew. Midrash – Song of Songs Rabba 4:5:2

'Moshe' is how the English name 'Moses' is pronounced in Hebrew.

I want to add a special thanks to Martin for his support, to Steve for the many ways he helped to get this book published, to my grandchildren for bringing great joy into my life, and to the Holy One, Blessed Be He, for creating us and bringing us to this day.